Early Childhood

# BIG BOOK of Bible Story Coloring Pages

DAVID C COOK
transforming lives together

BIG BOOK OF BIBLE STORY COLORING PAGES FOR EARLY CHILDHOOD
Published by David C Cook
4050 Lee Vance Drive
Colorado Springs, CO 80918 U.S.A.

Integrity Music Limited, a Division of David C Cook
Brighton, East Sussex BN1 2RE, England



ISBN 978-0-8307-7232-2



The content included in this book was originally published in *Thru-the-Bible Coloring Pages ages 3-6* by Standard Publishing in 2005 © Standard Publishing, ISBN 978-0-7847-1783-7.

Cover Design: James Hershberger
Illustrator: Janet Skiles

Printed in the United States of America

6 7 8 9 10 11 12 13 14 15

101424

# Contents

## New Testament

## Bible Memory Coloring Pages

# Introduction

*Big Book of Bible Story Coloring Pages for Early Childhood* includes Bible story pictures, application pictures, and memory verse pictures that correlate to the most popular Bible lessons for young children.

A Bible story coloring page provides a quick and easy way to introduce a Bible story or help children review the story. Most of the application coloring pages feature modern-day children and will help young learners take the Bible lesson home. The memory verse coloring pages use simple and shortened verses that young children can easily remember and use.

Young children are still developing their fine motor skills. Their drawings are more like scribbles because they are experimenting with crayons on paper rather than working toward a finished piece. Many young children are not capable of coloring within the lines or filling in every space on the page. Encourage children to keep exploring as you help them have fun "coloring" and learning about Bible things.

Guided conversation is important in making any activity a Bible-learning activity. Use conversation about the coloring page the child is working on to focus the child's thoughts on retelling the Bible story, naming ways to follow the example in the picture, or remembering helpful Bible words.

While a simple coloring activity is fun for many young children, consider making it part of a more active learning experience. The following pages suggest ways to use coloring pages in age-appropriate learning activities for young children.

# Bible Learning Activities with Coloring Pages

## More Than Just Crayons

Fat crayons for the very youngest artist are a great choice. Also consider providing sidewalk chalk. To use finger paints, copy the coloring pages on coated paper so the paint won't absorb into the paper quickly and the child has time to be creative.

## Touch-and-Feel Pictures

Copy the coloring page and mount each child's page on poster board or cardstock. Provide one or more of the following items for children to glue to their pictures: rice, beans, cotton, glitter, fabric, felt, popped popcorn.

## Dry Rice Pictures

You will need four cups uncooked rice, food coloring (red, green, blue, yellow), plastic bags, wax paper, four bowls, poster board or cardstock, glue. Put five drops of food coloring in each bag. Add one cup of rice to each bag. Seal and shake the bag to coat the rice. Pour the dyed rice onto wax paper and allow it to dry. Put dried rice into bowls. Copy a coloring page for each child and mount each page on poster board or cardstock. Children glue the dyed rice to their coloring pages.

## Classroom Big Book

Use a large piece of poster board for each page of the book. Allow children to choose what kind of book to make, or provide each child a coloring page based on your teaching theme. Give children time to color their pages, and then mount one page on each piece of poster board. Ask each child to dictate a sentence or two for his or her page in the book. Print the child's dictation under the picture, and let the child finish the page with a border, stickers, or fun designs. Put the big book together with three large rings. Have fun reading the book together.

## Thematic Bulletin Board

Choose coloring pages based on a teaching theme. (See the index for Bible themes.) Let the children color the pages, and add them to a bulletin board with an appropriate title. Consider cutting off the caption of the coloring page and allowing each child to dictate a sentence about the picture. Take pictures of your students, and display each child's picture and name beside his or her coloring page. A bulletin board mounted low on the wall would be ideal for this activity.

## Bible Lesson Visual

Choose a coloring page that illustrates a story or application you want to teach. Enlarge the picture, and enlist the help of older children to color it appropriately. Mount it and cover it with clear adhesive covering. Use the picture to introduce or review a story, or use the picture

to talk about the lesson application. It will be sturdy enough for young children to hold and pass around the story circle.

## Personal Coloring Books

Choose coloring pages based on the theme you are teaching. Copy about ten different pages for each child. Make each child a personal coloring book: use staples, yarn, or folders to keep the pages together. Let the children take their books home, and encourage family coloring fun and Bible learning at home.

## Memory Verse Poster

Choose an appropriate Bible verse coloring page, and make a copy for each child. Let each child color the verse page and then mount the page on construction paper. Adding borders of popped popcorn, stickers, or fingerprints makes the posters fun! Encourage children (and parents) to hang the poster in the child's room or play area.

## Puzzles

Copy, color, and mount on cardstock a coloring page that correlates to your teaching theme. Depending on the age of your students, cut the page into puzzle pieces (4–6 pieces for the youngest, 10–12 pieces for older children). Keep the pieces in a large resealable bag with an uncut coloring page. Many children will enjoy placing the pieces on the uncut page; others will want to work the puzzle without the uncut page.

## Place Mats

For special days and holidays, children can make place mats with coloring pages. Choose an appropriate picture to copy for each child. Pictures of creation work well for Thanksgiving, pictures of Jesus' birth certainly work for Christmas, and pictures of mothers or fathers with children work for Mother's Day and Father's Day. After children have colored their pages, mount each on a large sheet of construction paper, leaving room on one side for writing. Allow each child to dictate a sentence about the picture. Print the child's sentence on his or her construction paper. (Examples: "We celebrate Christmas because Jesus was born." "Thank You, God, for fruit." "Thank You, God, for my mother.") After children finish decorating their place mats, cover them with clear adhesive covering.

## Prayer Time

Choose coloring pages that correlate to your teaching theme, or choose coloring pages that show a variety of things that show God's care. Display the pages and use them to focus the children's thoughts for prayer time. You might say: "This picture shows something that God made. Thank You, God, for fruit. Ethan, what would you like to thank God for this morning?" Or, "This picture shows a way that God cares for us. Megan, how does God care for you? Let's thank God right now."

## Act It Out

Choose coloring pages that illustrate ways to help others. Display one page on each wall of the room. Travel with your children to the first wall. Talk about the picture, and then ask everyone to act it out with a friend. Continue traveling around the room and acting out each picture.

## Beanbag Game

Tape together four to eight coloring pages that correlate to stories the children have learned. Place the grouped pictures on the floor. Give each child a turn to throw a beanbag at one of the pages and tell something about that Bible story.

## Christmas Ornament

Copy the coloring page of baby Jesus for each child. Reduce as necessary to make sure the picture will fit on a margarine tub lid. Let the children color the picture and glue it to a margarine lid. Punch a hole in each lid, and attach a gold cord. Put green or red construction paper or felt on the other side of the lid. Older children may want to add glitter around the edge of the ornament.

## Mail It Home

For absentees or as a fun way to contact visitors, mail the coloring pages home with a note to the child. Children love to get mail, especially mail with a special activity to complete.

## Matching Game

Choose a coloring page that correlates to the Bible lesson. Color one copy of the page, and leave one copy uncolored. Attach the uncolored page to one side of a file folder. On the other side, make a pocket large enough to hold cutouts from the colored page. Cut objects and people from the colored page and put them into the pocket. Children will have fun pulling out an object and matching it to the same object on the uncolored page.

Genesis 1

# God Made the Sky and Earth

God made the sky and the earth.

Genesis 1

**God Made Fish and Birds**

God made fish and birds.

Genesis 1

**God Made Animals**

**God made all the animals.**

Genesis 1

## God Made a World for People

God made the world.

Genesis 1–2

## God Made People

God made people.

Genesis 1–2

**God Made Adam and Eve**

**God made people.**

Genesis 1–2; Proverbs 20

**God Made My Senses**

God made people special.

Genesis 1–2; Psalms 8, 139; Matthew 10

**God Made Me Special**

God made each of us special.

Geneisis 6–7

**Noah Builds a Boat**

God wants us to obey Him.

Genesis 7–9

**Noah and the Flood**

**God cares for us.**

Genesis 12

## Abram Moves

God wants us to follow Him.

Genesis 13

## Abram and Lot

God wants us to make good choices.

Genesis 17–18, 21

**Abraham and Sarah Have a Baby**

**God cares for families.**

Genesis 37, 39

**Joseph as a Boy**

God cares for us all the time.

Genesis 39, 41–42, 45, 47

**Joseph Serves God All His Life**

**God wants us to serve Him.**

Exodus 2

**Moses Is Born**

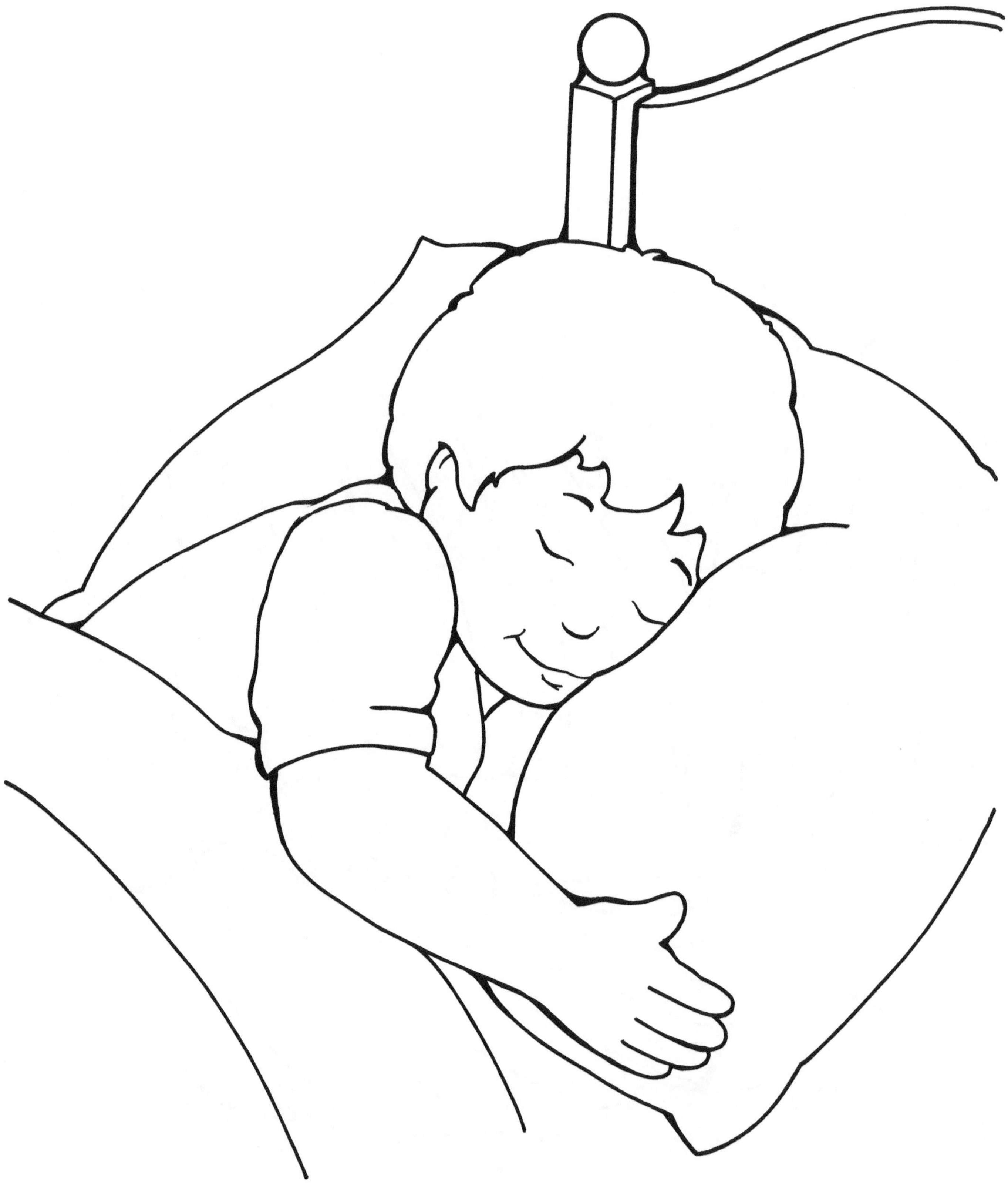

God cares for us.

Exodus 3, 7–13

**Moses Leads God's People**

God is always with us.

Exodus 13–15

**God's People Cross the Red Sea**

God helps us when we are afraid.

Exodus 16–17

**God Provides for His People**

**God gives us what we need.**

Exodus 19–20, 24, 32

**God Gives Ten Rules**

**God gives us good rules to obey.**

Numbers 13–14

**Joshua and Caleb**

**God is powerful. He will help us.**

Joshua 1, 3–4

**God's People Cross the Jordan River**

**God is powerful. He is with us.**

Joshua 6

**The Fall of Jericho**

God is powerful. We should obey Him.

Joshua 24

# Joshua Talks to God's People

**God is powerful. We can serve Him.**

Judges 6–7

**Gideon Leads God's Army**

God helps us obey Him.

Ruth 1–2

## Ruth Makes Good Choices

God helps us make good choices.

1 Samuel 1–3

**Samuel as a Boy**

God uses people to care for us.

1 Samuel 3, 8–10, 12

**Samuel Serves God All His Life**

God wants us to be His helpers.

1 Samuel 16

## David Plays for Saul

God wants us to help others.

1 Samuel 17

**David Meets Goliath**

God helps us be brave.

1 Samuel 18, 20

**David and Jonathan**

**God wants us to be good friends.**

2 Samuel 9

# David and Mephibosheth

**God wants us to be kind.**

2 Samuel 22; Psalms 4–5, 23, 100, 122, 150

**David Sings to God**

We can sing to God.

1 Kings 3–4

**Solomon Prays to Know What Is Right**

**We can ask God to help us know right from wrong.**

1 Kings 5–8

**Solomon Builds the Temple**

**We can worship God.**

1 Kings 17

**Elijah Is Fed by Ravens**

**God cares for us.**

1 Kings 17

**Elijah Helps a Widow**

**God wants us to obey Him.**

1 Kings 17

## Elijah Helps a Widow's Son

God listens to our prayers.

1 Kings 18

**Elijah and the Prophets of Baal**

**God is powerful.**

2 Kings 4

**Elisha and a Widow's Oil**

**God wants us to help others.**

2 Kings 4

**Elisha and a Shunammite Family**

God wants us to share with others.

2 Kings 4

**Elisha and the Shunammite's Son**

God has power to help us.

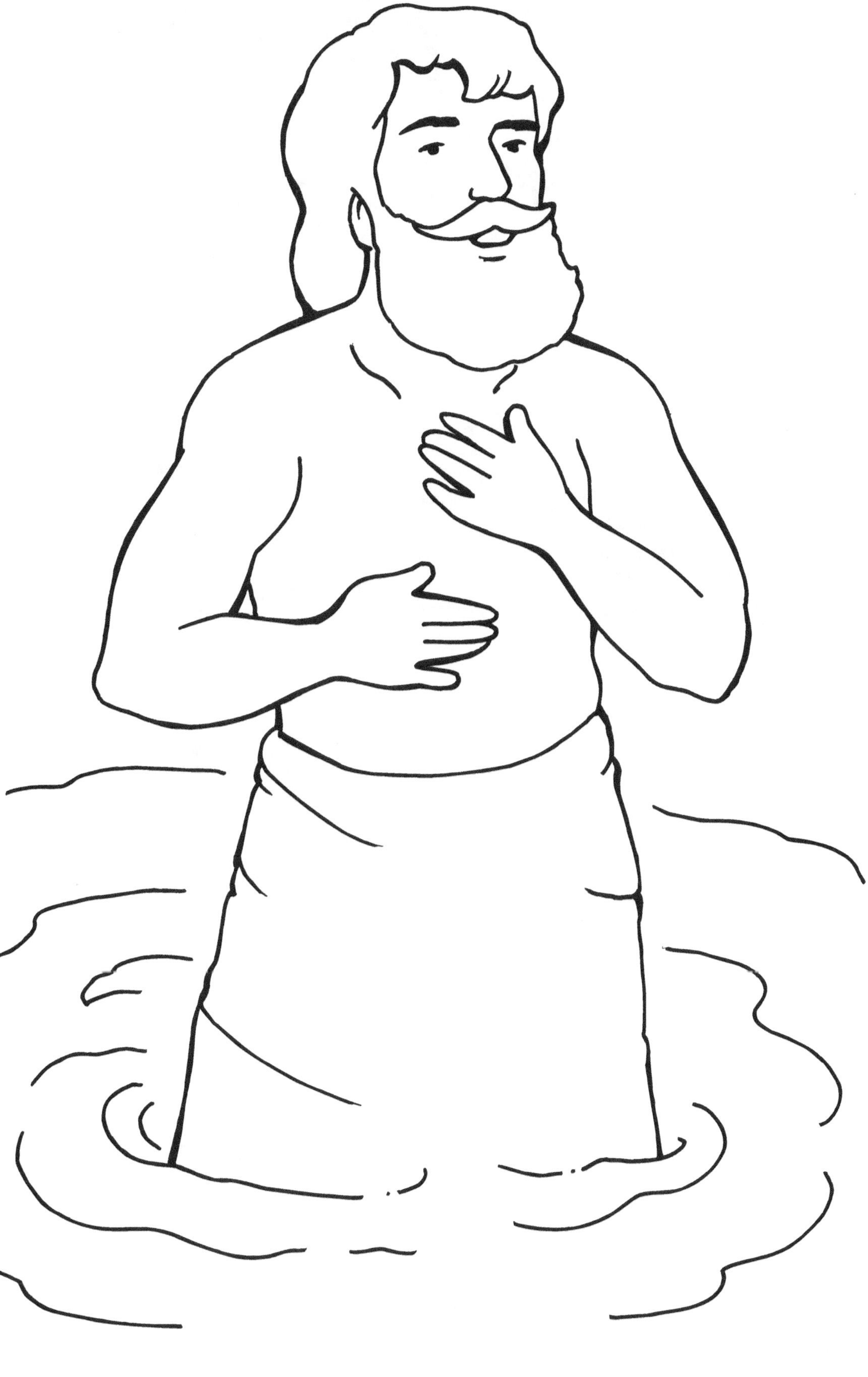

2 Kings 5

**Elisha and Naaman**

God want us to worship Him.

2 Kings 22–23

**Josiah Reads God's Word**

We can listen to God's Word.

2 Chronicles 17, 20

**Jehoshaphat Asks for God's Help**

We can ask God for His help.

Nehemiah 1–2, 4, 6

**Nehemiah Rebuilds the Wall**

God helps us all the time.

Esther 2–5, 7–8

## Esther Helps God's People

God helps us to help others.

Daniel 1

**Daniel and His Friends Obey God**

**We can obey God.**

Daniel 3

## Daniel's Friends Worship Only God

We can worship God.

Daniel 5

**Daniel and the Handwriting on the Wall**

We can tell about God.

Daniel 6

**Daniel and the Lions' Den**

We can pray to God.

Jonah 1–3

**Jonah Tells about God**

God helps us tell about Him.

Matthew 1; Luke 1

**An Angel Announces Jesus' Birth**

We can share good news about Jesus.

Matthew 1; Luke 1

## An Angel Brings Special News

**Jesus was a special baby.**

Luke 1–2

**Jesus Is Born**

We are happy Jesus was born.

Luke 2

**A Special Baby Is Born**

We are happy and thankful Jesus was born.

Luke 2

## Shepherds Hear Special News

We can tell others Jesus is special.

Luke 2

## Shepherds Visit Jesus

We can tell others Jesus was born.

Luke 2

## Simeon and Anna See Jesus

**We are thankful Jesus was born.**

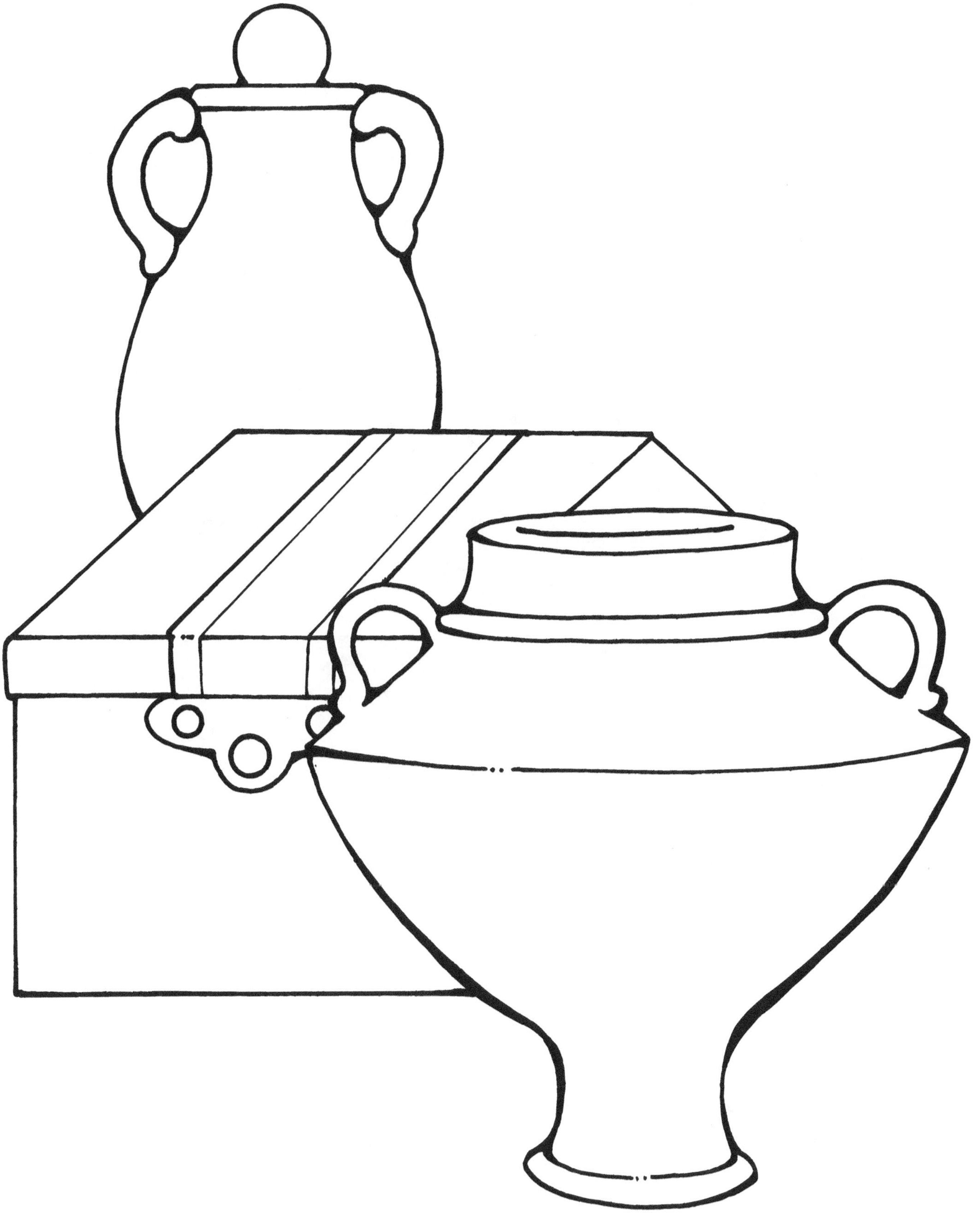

Matthew 2

# Wise Men Worship a Special Baby

We can worship Jesus.

Matthew 2

# Wise Men Worship Jesus

We can worship Jesus.

Luke 2

## Jesus as a Boy

Jesus pleased God.

Matthew 3; Mark 1

**Jesus Is Baptized**

We can please God.

Matthew 4

**Jesus Is Tempted**

God's Word helps us do what is right.

John 1

**Two Friends Follow Jesus**

Jesus wants us to tell about Him.

John 4

**Jesus and a Woman from Samaria**

Jesus loves people everywhere.

John 4

**Jesus Heals an Official's Son**

**Jesus does great things.**

Matthew 4

**Jesus Begins to Teach**

We can tell about Jesus.

Luke 5

## Fishermen Follow Jesus

Jesus wants us to obey Him.

Mark 2; Luke 5

**Jesus Heals a Man Who Could Not Walk**

Jesus always helps us.

Matthew 9; Luke 5

## Jesus and Matthew

Jesus loves all people.

Matthew 5–7

# Jesus Teaches about Pleasing God

We can please God.

Matthew 6; Mark 12

# Jesus Teaches about Giving

We can give to God.

Matthew 8; Luke 7

**Jesus Heals the Soldier's Servant**

Jesus has power to heal people.

Luke 7

**Jesus Brings a Young Man Back to Life**

Jesus always cares for us.

Mark 4

## Jesus Stops a Storm

Jesus has power to stop a storm.

Luke 8

**Jesus Heals a Young Girl**

**Jesus has power to help families.**

John 6

**Jesus Feeds a Crowd**

Jesus has power to give us what we need.

Mark 6; John 6

**Jesus Walks on Water**

Jesus has power to walk on water.

Mark 7

## Jesus Heals a Man Who Could Not Hear or Speak

Jesus can help us because He is the Son of God.

John 9

# Jesus Heals a Man Born Blind

Jesus has power to help people.

Matthew 7; Luke 10

## Jesus Teaches about Helping

We can help others.

Luke 10

## Mary and Martha Follow Jesus

Jesus wants us to learn about Him.

Matthew 6; Luke 11

**Jesus Teaches about Praying**

We can pray to God.

Luke 12

## Jesus Teaches about Sharing

We can share with others.

John 11

# Jesus Brings Lazarus Back to Life

Jesus is God's Son.

Luke 17

## Jesus Heals Ten Men

Jesus has power to heal people.

Mark 10

**Jesus and the Children**

**Jesus loves children.**

Mark 10; Luke 18

**Bartimaeus Follows Jesus**

Jesus wants us to follow Him.

Luke 19

# Jesus and Zacchaeus

**Jesus wants us to love others.**

Matthew 21

# A Crowd Welcomes Jesus

We can praise Jesus.

Mark 11

**People Praise Jesus**

We can praise Jesus.

Matthew 28

**Jesus Is Alive!**

Jesus is alive!

John 21

**Jesus Lives!**

Jesus is alive!

Acts 2

**Peter Preaches about Jesus**

**We can follow Jesus.**

Acts 2, 4

**The Church Follows Jesus**

We can share with friends at church.

Acts 3

**Peter and John at the Temple**

We learn about Jesus from other people.

Acts 8

## Philip Tells about Jesus

We learn about Jesus from the Bible.

Acts 9

# Saul Begins to Follow Jesus

We can follow Jesus.

Acts 9

**Peter and Tabitha**

**We can help others learn about Jesus.**

Acts 12

## The Church Prays for Peter in Prison

We can pray for people who tell about Jesus.

Acts 16

**Lydia Follows Jesus**

We can learn about Jesus.

Acts 16

## The Jailer Follows Jesus

We can sing and tell about Jesus.

Acts 28; Ephesians 4, 6; Philippians 1–2; Colossians 4

**Paul Helps People Follow Jesus**

**We can tell about Jesus.**

Genesis 1:1

**"God created the sky and the earth."**

Genesis 17:1

**"Obey me and do what is right."**

Deuteronomy 6:5

**"Love ... God with all your heart."**

Deuteronomy 6:18
**"Do what the Lord says is good and right."**

Joshua 24:24

**"We will serve the Lord our God."**

Psalm 105:1

**“Give thanks to the Lord and pray to him.”**

Psalm 119:10

**“With all my heart I try to obey you, God.”**

Psalm 124:8

**"Our help comes from the Lord."**

Psalm 139:14

**“I praise you because you made me.”**

Psalm 147:5

**"Our Lord is great and very powerful."**

Proverbs 17:17

**"A friend loves you all the time."**

Matthew 2:1–2

**"Jesus was born.... 'We came to worship him.'"**

Matthew 4:19

**"Jesus said, 'Come follow me.'"**

Matthew 16:16

**"You are ... the Son of ... God."**

Luke 2:10–11

**“I am bringing you some good news.... Today your Savior was born.”**

Luke 2:52

**"Jesus continued to learn more and more ... and he pleased God."**

John 14:23

**"Jesus answered, ... 'Obey my teaching.'"**

Acts 5:42

**"Tell the Good News—that Jesus is the Christ."**

1 John 4:7

**"Love each other ... love comes from God."**

# Index

HeartShaper — Shaping Hearts with God's Word

# Preschool/Pre-K & K Scope & Sequence

## Fall Year 1

- God Made the Sky and Earth (pp. 11–12)
- God Made Fish and Birds (pp. 13–14)
- God Made Animals (pp. 15–16)
- God Made People (pp. 19–20)
- Noah Builds a Boat (pp. 27–28)
- Noah and the Flood (pp. 29–30)
- Abram Moves (pp. 31–32)
- Abram and Lot (pp. 33–34)
- Abraham and Sarah Have a Baby (pp. 35–36)
- Joseph as a Boy (pp. 37–38)
- Joseph Serves God All His Life (pp. 39–40)
- Samuel as a Boy (pp. 63–64)
- Samuel Serves God All His Life (pp. 65–66)

## Winter Year 1

- An Angel Announces Jesus' Birth (pp. 115–116)
- Jesus Is Born (pp. 119–120)
- Shepherds Visit Jesus (pp. 125–126)
- Simeon and Anna See Jesus (pp. 127–128)
- Wise Men Worship Jesus (pp. 131–132)
- Jesus as a Boy (pp. 133–134)
- Jesus Is Baptized (pp. 135–136)
- Jesus Is Tempted (pp. 137–138)
- Jesus Begins to Teach (pp. 145–146)
- Jesus and the Children (pp. 185–186)
- Jesus and Matthew (pp. 151–152)
- Jesus and a Woman from Samaria (pp. 141–142)
- Jesus and Zacchaeus (pp. 189–190)

## Spring Year 1

- Triumphal Entry: People Praise Jesus (pp. 193–194)
- Resurrection Sunday: Jesus Lives! (pp. 197–198)
- Jesus Heals an Official's Son (pp. 143–144)
- Jesus Heals a Man Who Could Not Walk (pp. 149–150)
- Jesus Heals the Soldier's Servant (pp. 157–158)
- Jesus Brings a Young Man Back to Life (pp. 159–160)
- Jesus Walks on Water (pp. 167–168)
- Jesus Heals a Man Who Could Not Hear or Speak (pp. 169–170)
- Peter Preaches about Jesus (pp. 199–200)
- Peter and John at the Temple (pp. 203–204)
- Philip Tells about Jesus (pp. 205–206)
- Peter and Tabitha (pp. 209–210)
- The Church Prays for Peter in Prison (pp. 211–212)

## Summer Year 1

- David Plays for Saul (pp. 67–68)
- David Meets Goliath (pp. 69–70)
- David and Jonathan (pp. 71–72)
- David and Mephibosheth (pp. 73–74)
- David Sings to God (pp. 75–76)
- Solomon Prays to Know What Is Right (pp. 77–78)
- Solomon Builds the Temple (pp. 79–80)
- Jehoshaphat Asks for God's Help (pp. 99–100)
- Josiah Reads God's Word (pp. 97–98)
- Elisha and a Widow's Oil (pp. 89–90)
- Elisha and a Shunammite Family (pp. 91–92)
- Elisha and the Shunammite's Son (pp. 93–94)
- Elisha and Naaman (pp. 95–96)

### BIBLE Memory

*Fall Year 1*
- Unit 1: Genesis 1:1 (p. 219)
- Unit 2: Genesis 17:1 (p. 220)

*Winter Year 1*
- Unit 1: Matthew 2:1–2 (p. 230)
- Unit 2: Luke 2:52 (p. 234)
- Unit 3: 1 John 4:7 (p. 237)

*Spring Year 1*
- Unit 1: Psalm 147:5 (p. 228)
- Unit 2: Acts 5:42 (p. 236)

*Summer Year 1*
- Unit 1: Proverbs 17:17 (p. 229)
- Unit 2: Deuteronomy 6:5 (p. 221)
- Unit 3: Psalm 124:8 (p. 226)

## Fall Year 2
- God Made a World for People (pp. 17–18)
- God Made Adam and Eve (pp. 21–22)
- God Made My Senses (pp. 23–24)
- God Made Me Special (pp. 25–26)
- Moses Is Born (pp. 41–42)
- Moses Leads God's People (pp. 43–44)
- God's People Cross the Red Sea (pp. 45–46)
- God Provides for His People (pp. 47–48)
- God Gives Ten Rules (pp. 49–50)
- Joshua and Caleb (pp. 51–52)
- God's People Cross the Jordan River (pp. 53–54)
- The Fall of Jericho (pp. 55–56)
- Joshua Talks to God's People (pp. 57–58)

## Winter Year 2
- An Angel Brings Special News (pp. 117–118)
- A Special Baby Is Born (pp. 121–122)
- Shepherds Hear Special News (pp. 123–124)
- Wise Men Worship a Special Baby (pp. 129–130)
- Jesus Teaches about Pleasing God (pp. 153–154)
- Jesus Teaches about Giving (pp. 155–156)
- Jesus Teaches about Praying (pp. 177–178)
- Jesus Teaches about Helping (pp. 173–174)
- Jesus Teaches about Sharing (pp. 179–180)
- Two Friends Follow Jesus (pp. 139–140)
- Fishermen Follow Jesus (pp. 147–148)
- Mary and Martha Follow Jesus (pp. 175–176)
- Bartimaeus Follows Jesus (pp. 187–188)

## Spring Year 2
- Triumphal Entry: A Crowd Welcomes Jesus (pp. 191–192)
- Resurrection Sunday: Jesus Is Alive! (pp. 195–196)
- Jesus Stops a Storm (pp. 161–162)
- Jesus Heals a Young Girl (pp. 163–164)
- Jesus Feeds a Crowd (pp. 165–166)
- Jesus Heals a Man Born Blind (pp. 171–172)
- Jesus Heals Ten Men (pp. 183–184)
- Jesus Brings Lazarus Back to Life (pp. 181–182)
- The Church Follows Jesus (pp. 201–202)
- Saul Begins to Follow Jesus (pp. 207–208)
- Lydia Follows Jesus (pp. 213–214)
- The Jailer Follows Jesus (pp. 215–216)
- Paul Helps People Follow Jesus (pp. 217–218)

## Summer Year 2
- Elijah Is Fed by Ravens (pp. 81–82)
- Elijah Helps a Widow (pp. 83–84)
- Elijah Helps a Widow's Son (pp. 85–86)
- Elijah and the Prophets of Baal (pp. 87–88)
- Daniel and His Friends Obey God (pp. 105–106)
- Daniel's Friends Worship Only God (pp. 107–108)
- Daniel and the Handwriting on the Wall (pp. 109–110)
- Daniel and the Lions' Den (pp. 111–112)
- Gideon Leads God's Army (pp. 59–60)
- Ruth Makes Good Choices (pp. 61–62)
- Jonah Tells about God (pp. 113–114)
- Esther Helps God's People (pp. 103–104)
- Nehemiah Rebuilds the Wall (pp. 101–102)

### BIBLE Memory
*Fall Year 2*
- Unit 1: Psalm 139:14 (p. 227)
- Unit 2: Psalm 105:1 (p. 224)
- Unit 3: Joshua 24:24 (p. 223)

*Winter Year 2*
- Unit 1: Luke 2:10–11 (p. 233)
- Unit 2: John 14:23 (p. 235)
- Unit 3: Matthew 4:19 (p. 231)

*Spring Year 2*
- Special Unit: Matthew 16:16 (p. 232)
- Unit 1: Psalm 147:5 (p. 228)

*Summer Year 2*
- Unit 2: Psalm 119:10 (p. 225)
- Unit 3: Deuteronomy 6:18 (p. 222)